Money Stacking Habits

Habits to Better Manage Your Money and Your Finances

Jeffrey A. Holmes

Copyrights

All rights reserved © 2017 Jeffrey A. Holmes. No part of this publication or the information in it may be quoted from or reproduced in any form by means such as printing, scanning, photocopying, or otherwise without prior written permission of the copyright holder.

Disclaimer and Terms of Use

Effort has been made to ensure that the information in this book is accurate and complete. However, the author and the publisher do not warrant the accuracy of the information, text, and graphics contained within the book due to the rapidly changing nature of science, research, known and unknown facts and internet. The Author and the publisher do not hold any responsibility for errors, omissions or contrary interpretation of the subject matter herein. This book is presented solely for motivational and informational purposes

Printed in the United States
ISBN: 978-1975853792

Contents

Introduction	1
Work	5
The Need to Develop Money Stacking Habits	7
25 Money Stacking Habits You Should Develop	15
Steps to Building Habits	71
The Warren Buffet Example	77
Conclusion	83

Introduction

Money is obviously a very important part of our everyday lives. More than that, money is arguably the single most powerful force in the world. Everything we need to survive is directly linked to money, and many of the things that make us happy are also somehow connected to money. Even if you believe that the most important things in life are love and family, the bottom line is that these are often unattainable in the absence of money. How will you get married and maintain a family if you don't have money? How will you support your spouse or take care of a sick child if there is no money?

Money can be simply defined as legal tender in exchange for goods and services. It is a verifiable and accepted means of payment within a country. People have been exchanging goods and services from the beginning of time, but the concept of money was first developed around 3000 BC in Mesopotamia.

Before this, the trade by barter system was the normal way of effecting transactions. In this system, an individual has item A but needs item B. Another individual has item B but needs item A. They locate each other and make an exchange. In more complicated scenarios, individuals with item C and/or D might be involved, where the first individual with item A needs item B, the second individual with item B needs item C, the third individual with item C needs item D and the fourth individual with item D needs item A.

It's easy to see the difficulty of transacting with this system. In the above scenario, what happens if the first three individuals cannot find anyone with item D who needs item A? The optimum trade will be impossible, and they will either not transact at all or be forced to accept an item they don't really need in the hope that they can trade it for something useful later.

There is also the problem of value with the trade by barter system. Say I have made a chair worth 15 baskets and I need a basket. If I want to exchange, I will have to collect 15 baskets, even though I need just one, or I will be forced to exchange the much more valuable chair for one basket.

The development of money made it possible for people to get only things they need, in the actual quantity they need them.

Under the trade by barter system, it only made sense to produce everyday necessities. People made their living as farmers, tailors, and carpenters because it was easy to exchange the goods they made. However, commodities which people needed only occasionally were scarce. With the introduction of money, it became more feasible to engage in more specialized professions. A skilled professional could now sell his goods or services not only to those who had something he needed, but to anyone who had money to pay him. He could then use the money to buy whatever he needed – or wanted.

Money is now used all over the world. Most countries have their own currency, and there are also instances where a number of countries have agreed to use the same currency to transact business. Examples include the Eurozone and a number of Central African countries using the Franc. There are a few other regions that are trying to introduce a central currency, such as the Economic Community of West African States (ECOWAS), which is trying to introduce a single currency, the Eco, for use among member countries. The aim of a unified currency is to encourage trade among countries, much like money itself encourages trade among individuals.

There are now many currencies that are recognized all over the world, and once you have money, you can get any goods or services you desire. When you travel to a foreign country, you can easily get your money exchanged to the currency of that country and pay for goods and services there as well.

The ease with which money can be spent, however, comes with a challenge: saving. Most people find it very difficult to make money and very easy to spend it. Actually, saving money requires a very high level of discipline.

If you like to read financial books, articles, or blogs, chances are that you've come across the phrase 'Stack your Money and Act Broke'. Stack in this case refers to a sum of $1,000. The importance of this figure lies in the fact that unexpected emergencies are an inevitable part of life – and it is calculated that about two-thirds of Americans would find an emergency costing above $1,000 very difficult to take care of. For some people, even a $100 emergency could be a very big problem.

Apart from accidents and illness that could lead to the sudden need for money, there is also the issue of job loss. Losing a job is always stressful, but having some money in the bank will save you a lot of worry. You will be aware that you can go on meeting your basic expenses for the next few months. You will be more relaxed, and will be able to make a more informed and beneficial decision about your next position, rather than just taking the first job that comes along because you're desperate for cash.

Work

Work can be defined as an activity we carry out in exchange for payments in the form of money. However, even in modern times, there are still a few occasions where people work in exchange for payments in kind, which is related to trade by barter. Recent technological advancements have created a huge variety of jobs, which are generally grouped into 'low skill' and 'skilled'. The type of job an individual is able to take is usually tied to their educational background, skills and working experience.

Low skill workers are those who have never had any formal education or who have low educational attainment – typically a high school diploma at most. They often receive the lowest wages as well. They are a major part of the general labor market. Their jobs often consist of repetitive or menial tasks, and most of these jobs can be completely learnt in 30 days or less. Low skill workers can be further divided into 'unskilled' and 'semi-skilled' workers.

A skilled worker is someone who can work efficiently with little supervision and make some level of independent judgments. Such people are usually well educated, with a minimum of an undergraduate degree. They may have several years of experience in their skilled profession, as well as higher degrees and professional certifications. They also supervise other skilled and unskilled workers to ensure that their jobs are efficiently carried out.

A skilled worker will normally earn more than a low skill worker. Since the amount you earn determines how much you can save, continuous self-development is highly recommended. This is irrespective of your current skill level. As you develop your skills, it becomes easier to position yourself for better paying jobs and the ability to save more. Many people lose their chance at a better paying job simply because they do not have the right qualifications or experience.

The Need to Develop Money Stacking Habits

There are a lot of people with the (incorrect) mentality that money is meant to be spent. They end up spending all they earn before their next pay check. While money is indeed meant to be spent, it is important that it be spent wisely. It is also important to put some aside. There are many benefits to saving. You will still end up spending the money at some point, but you will be getting much more value for it.

Here are some reasons why you should adopt money stacking habits.

Financial Independence

You'll certainly get a lot of different answers if you ask people what it means to be rich. The common denominator in all of the definitions, however, will be the ability to take care of all your financial needs without having to borrow money. This is only possible when you have savings. Before you can be financially independent, you must have some money you can use for non-basic activities without needing to pull out a credit card and without emptying your bank account. These activities could include taking a job that pays less but offers you more satisfaction, helping members of your family, or investing in a start-up business run by someone else. Other examples could be starting a business of your own, going back to school, retiring early, or going on a vacation. While having financial independence does not exactly mean being rich, it is a prerequisite to being rich. And aside from factors like the type of car you drive and the size of your house, the confidence and comfort you get from having substantial savings to fall back on can really make you feel like a rich man!

Reduces Your Expenses

Saving can go a very long way to help you reduce your expenses. Considering how easy it is to get access to credit cards and other forms of credit, a lot of people are spending as much as double when buying goods. They buy something on credit, can't pay it off right away, and then have to pay the accrued interest as well as the original purchase price. Saving up for what you need prior to buying it will eliminate these interest payments.

Having some savings also gives you the opportunity to buy things at a cheaper price. Suppose you come upon a clearance sale. If you have money saved up, you can easily use some of it to buy sale items that you know you'll need in the future. You'll actually end up saving more than you would have spent when you eventually had to buy the item.

For example, imagine you have $1,000 in your savings account and you usually buy groceries on a monthly basis. You spend $100 every month on groceries. If you get to the store and find out that they are giving a 24% discount on groceries, it means that for this month you can buy your groceries for just $76. And because of your savings, you can also buy for five months in advance, which will come to $380. (Of course, this means buying canned goods and other groceries that won't expire within the next five to six months.) You will have saved $120. For each of the next five months, you can add the $76 you pulled out to your normal savings. You might even decide to save the entire $100 you would have spent on groceries for each month; or you could divide the $24 you are saving into two – $12 to your savings and the other $12 to reward yourself.

There are also times when your savings can help you get normally expensive items at a very cheap price. Imagine you hear of someone who has a car worth $10,000 and an urgent need for $5,000. He has decided to sell his car, probably as a last resort to raise the money. He might be willing to accept $7,500 – or even $5,000 – the car, depending on his level of need. If you have that much in your savings account, you will be able to get the car at a cheaper price. Even if you don't need a car, you might decide to buy this car for $5,000 and then sell it to someone for its fair market value. For just that transaction, you could easily make over $3,000, which can fully or partially go back to your savings (along with the $5,000 you pulled out to buy the car).

To Buy a House or a Car

If you need to buy a house or a car, you will need some form of down payment before a bank will loan you the rest of the money. Most financial institutions will require a minimum 5% down payment and another 5% for extra expenses. That means you'll have to save some money.

Your savings toward a house or a car should be separate from your savings for retirement or emergency purposes. This is to avoid getting stranded just after making a down payment. You don't want to have an emergency come up just when you have no cash on hand and a new mortgage or car loan eating up your disposable income!

To Avoid Debt

If you want to live debt-free, then you will have to save some money. If you are always using your credit card for every emergency or unplanned expense that comes up, you'll always be in some amount of debt. No matter how much we plan, we still encounter unexpected expenses every month. Imagine your car suddenly breaking down, or a neighborhood child hitting a baseball through your front window. In both cases, you will have to address the issue immediately, and this will mean spending some money you didn't plan for. That's why it's such a great idea to have a reserve fund for emergencies. The reserve fund could range between $500 and $1,000. This will help ensure you don't go into debt or suffer till your next paycheck when you have an emergency to take care of.

Annual Expenses

There are certain payments we have to make once or twice a year. For instance, if you own your home, you will have to pay property tax every year. Or think about your annual summer vacation trip, or gift giving at Christmastime. If you decide to wait until the last moment – or even a few months before – to start raising the money, you might not be able to do it.

The best option is to always begin saving for the next occurrence of such an expense from the moment you've paid for the last one. For an annual expense, this means spreading out the cost over an entire year. Say you pay $900 in property tax every year. It will be easier for you to start saving $75 every month, the instant you pay this year's tax, than trying to raise $450 twice in the two months before the next deadline.

Major Emergencies

Emergencies can come up at any time of the month or year. The problem with emergencies, however, is that they are expenses that cannot wait. You have to take care of the problem right away, or it could get worse – and even fatal. For instance, if your child suddenly falls ill and you don't have the money for the medication the doctor prescribes, recovery will certainly be delayed, and death may result, depending on the severity of the illness. To avoid this scenario, it vital to always have money in a savings account that you can use to take care of any expense that comes up.

Other emergencies that would need to be taken care of immediately could include your house getting flooded or burning down, a car accident, a lawsuit, and the funeral of a close friend or family member. Whatever the emergency that catches you unawares, it is always easier to deal with when you have some substantial savings that can cover the financial aspects of the situation.

Job Loss

When you're an expert in your field and everything is going well at work, you might be tempted to think that nothing could go wrong. However, a lot of people with secure jobs have learnt their lesson the hard way. The fact is that a company can suddenly close down or a department can be eliminated and everybody who works there can be laid off. And even if nothing happens to your job, what if you're seriously hurt or become too sick to work? Not only will you have to survive on your savings, you'll also have to pay for your treatment. Therefore, everybody needs to be prepared for job loss at all times.

Since you must have been unemployed for six weeks before you can access your unemployment insurance, you will need at least six weeks' worth of savings. If you don't have it, you'll be forced to start using up your credit. Imagine a situation where you had some outstanding debt before you lost your job, and you'll see what a problem that would be. Even if you were debt-free to begin with, you don't know how long it will take to find another job, or how much it will pay. The new debts you will have accrued will make it difficult for you to get your finances back on track for quite some time after you start working again.

Retirement

Everybody hopes for that day they can retire and enjoy a few years of rest before they finally bid the world goodbye. With improvements in technology, public health and medicine, people are living longer, but this does not mean that we will be strong enough to work all our lives – or that we'd want to. In line with this, it's a great idea to start saving for retirement the instant you start working. While saving for emergencies and for that dream house or car, you should be saving for your retirement as well. If you start saving for retirement the instant you start working, a savings of 5% or less per month should leave you with enough to live happily and satisfactorily after your retirement.

Health

Having savings actually helps you stay healthy. Not having savings has a way of eroding your peace of mind, which subsequently impacts your health. When you have no savings, you'll always have money worries. You'll be worried about what will happen if an emergency suddenly comes up and your credit card can't handle it. You'll be worried about suddenly losing your job, or about something going wrong with you or a family member. All of this worry negatively affects your health, leading to increased blood pressure and other problems. By the time something bad finally does happen, you'll be in such bad shape that you might end up having a heart attack!

25 Money Stacking Habits You Should Develop

To be able to save, you will need to develop some new habits. These habits will help you become conscious of saving money as well as how you spend money. The more you practice them, the more they will become a part of you over time. Within a short while, stacking money will become the new normal for you. The reason that many people find it difficult to begin stacking money is that the habits they practice encourage them to spend on everything they want to buy. They don't really think about how much they need it, or if they would be better off saving the money. Here are some habits you should consciously start developing if you intend to start saving money and enjoying the advantages of having savings:

1. Developing a Scale of reference

'Scale of preference' is an economic concept that entails arranging the items a person needs in terms of how important they are. This is a great way of putting a limit on the amount you spend every month.

Your typical list for a month could include drinking water, food, toiletries, clothes, a new pair of shoes, a new game for your PS4 and new light bulbs for your house. Suppose you plan to spend $100 for the month. Now arrange the items in order of importance, probably drinking water, food, toiletries, light bulbs, shoes, clothes and finally the videogame. Sum their costs, stopping once you reach $100. Those will be the things you will buy for the month. Other things can be pushed to the next month.

You can, of course, make some changes. For instance, if your $100 gets exhausted at toiletries and you really need to change the light bulbs, you might decide to skip the drinking water and just drink boiled tap water. Another alternative would be tweaking the price for each item. You might reduce the amount you will spend on water, food and toiletries so that more items make the cutoff.

This list is just an example; in real life you can be sure it will include several other things like transportation to and from work, friends asking for loans, rent, car payments, etc. If you are married, your expenses will double as you will have an extra person to care for, and once you have kids, you'll have to feed and clothe them too, as well as pay school fees.

You will therefore have to think far and wide while developing your scale of preference. This is to avoid a scenario where you have developed a budget and listed things to be paid for under that budget, only for other more important items to suddenly come up. If that happens when you have exhausted your budget, you will be forced to overspend, and before you know it, you'll be in debt.

One way to approach this is to keep a record of all your expenses during a particular month. This will become your reference while you are preparing your scale of preference for the next month. This will make it easy to capture recurring expenses, but you should also leave a substantial amount, say 10 to 20% of your budget, for emergency spending. This should cover any urgent expenses that come up.

Avoid the temptation to spend this emergency fund on unimportant items. Before buying something, make sure that it is more important than the lowest item on your scale of preference. Even then, you should still vet it to be sure that it is a need and not just a want. This is not an easy test to pass.

A need is something you require to lead a healthy life. When you are denied a need, the outcome will be so adverse that it could lead to physical dysfunction or even death. Some items that qualify as needs include air, food, water and shelter. Lack of any of these will kill you sooner or later – within a few minutes for air to about 40 days for food.

There are different types of needs. Food is an example of a physical and subjective need, while self-esteem is a subjective and psychological need. Other needs may be societal or social in nature.

Wants can also be described in many ways. Some are economic, while others are sociological or psychological, such as an emotional desire. Economically, a want is defined as an item that an individual desires. Wants are often considered to be unlimited. The implication is that you will never be able to buy everything you want, no matter how much you earn. If you are trying to buy everything you want, you will not be able to save, because you will be spending everything you earn – and you still won't have everything you want!

In differentiating between needs and wants, needs are items that you must have to survive. Wants are items that you desire to have because they are luxurious or fun; not having them will not directly impair your functionality.

Therefore, when you are developing your scale of preference, first consider all your needs for the month and allocate sufficient funds to them. Your wants can then follow in their order of importance.

2. Be aware of every cent you spend

Another money stacking habit you should develop is to be aware of every single cent you spend. It's much easier to get carried away while shopping if you don't realize how much you're spending. If you're always wondering how you spent all your money, you haven't been paying proper attention to your purchases. Perhaps you've found yourself in a situation where you left the house with $50 and returned expecting to find at least $40 in your pocket – only to find out that you had just $10 left. Hopefully you were able to figure out where the other $30 went, but some people end up unsure if they actually spent the money or if it just dropped out of their pocket!

To be aware of every cent you spend, you have to know what you will spend money on even before you leave the house in the morning. Try to carry no more cash than you will need for those important expenses you have budgeted for the day. This makes it much harder to overspend. Any other expenses that come up during that day will have to wait till tomorrow – or later. This gives you time to sleep on it and think about it, so you can decide whether you really need to spend that money. If it still seems like a necessity the following morning, then you can add it to what you are taking along that day. On the other hand, if you decide after you have thoroughly considered it that it's not worth it, you should put the money in your savings.

You will be amazed at how much you can save and how careful you will be if you develop the habit of being aware of how much you have spent.

Another great way to be aware of every cent that you spend is to keep a record of everything you buy. You might carry a small notepad where you can immediately jot down what you bought and how much you paid for it. At the end of the day, you can transfer these notes to a more permanent ledger or a computer spreadsheet. During the weekend or at the end of the month you can carry out a comprehensive review of everything you have spent and decide what was worth it and what wasn't. From there, you can make mental notes of expenses to avoid in the next week or month.

Money you save by refraining from your previous unnecessary purchases can be deposited in your savings. You should be able to save a significant sum every month if you are deliberate about your spending by being conscious of every cent you spend and ensuring that they are properly spent.

3. Do Not Live Above Your Income

A major temptation for many of us is living above our income. This is, however, the easiest way to get indebted. The world is full of items that catch our attention, and we often see the glamorous lives of celebrities and wish we could have what they have, or at least some of what they have. This is especially true in the case of celebrities that we particularly admire. Many brands take advantage of this, using our favorite celebrities as ambassadors for their products so as to tempt us to buy them. The idea is that when our favorite celebrity is their ambassador, our love for the ambassador will trickle down to their products and then we will love their products, hopefully enough to purchase them regularly. There is also peer pressure: We want what our friends and acquaintances are using.

All of these factors make it difficult for us to spend only what we can afford. We want to have the most expensive things that money can buy. We want to have the latest 100-inch curved 3D flat screen television that sells for $100,000 when we can get a 30-inch flat screen TV for less than $500. We want to live in mansions, even if we are single and a 1-bedroom apartment will serve us perfectly well. We all want to drive a brand-new Mercedes when an old Toyota Corolla would be cheaper and easier to maintain.

Considering how expensive it is to buy the best of everything, very few of us can actually afford it – and a good percentage of those who can know that it's not in their best interest to do so. As for the rest of us, the wise go for functionality and try to buy exactly what they can afford. Many others, though, try to keep up with the trends. They know they can't get the most expensive items, but they're quite willing to spring for brands that cost just a bit more than what they can actually afford.

Buying very expensive brands, however, is a sure path to money problems. Imagine using your life savings plus your salary for the current month to get a mobile phone when there are perfectly decent smartphones that cost just half of your salary. The major issue with this type of decision is that the expensive phones have almost exactly the same functionality as the cheaper ones. Even when the expensive ones have a few more features, they are often not really important – and in many cases not useful at all.

Mobile phones are just an example; this applies equally to expensive cosmetics, expensive perfumes, expensive clothes, expensive electronics, expensive houses and expensive cars. It is important to develop a habit of buying the cheapest item that has the functionality you need, as long as it is of reasonably high quality and its accessories and spare parts are readily available.

It is also worthy of note that items that are expensive to buy are also expensive to repair. The screen of a $5,000 phone will not be the same price as the screen of a phone worth $500. The same applies to every other spare part, as well as the labor cost for repairs. The tail light of some of the most expensive cars costs almost as much as some used vehicles. You should therefore be aware that the cost of buying an expensive item is not just limited to the initial price; the cost of maintaining it should also be considered. And what if it is lost or stolen? The replacement cost (or insurance premiums) will be very high as well.

Remember also that in the future you'll be able to get the equivalent of many of the things you want today much less expensively. You'll just have to sacrifice a little in the meantime. (The reason why I used 'equivalent' is that some things do become outdated; the best phones of 1997 aren't useful anymore, and the designs and functionalities look funny.) Saving – and investing what you have saved – could make several things that are currently beyond your means very affordable for you in the future.

Another way people live beyond their means is going on foreign trips, especially to very expensive countries. Virtually every country has its own tourist attractions that citizens can easily visit when they want to go on a vacation. This will be cheaper and less time consuming than going to a foreign country for the same purpose.

It's best to try to live below your income. This is the only way you can live comfortably throughout the month without getting into debt, and while still making regular contributions to your savings account.

The idea is this: If your monthly income is $5,000, you act as if you only earn $3,500 per month. You plan all of your monthly expenses and activities around that $3,500, while the $1,500 goes into your savings. By the end of the year, you will have saved $18,000, and after 10 years, you will have at least $180,000 in your account. Of course, if you are putting the money in a savings account, you will have gotten some interest on it. You may also have decided to invest some of it in profitable ventures that will have earned you even more. This is especially possible when you are able to save some of the $3,500 for other occasional and emergency expenses, such as buying a new car or going on a vacation.

4. Avoid Debt

Staying away from debt is another great money stacking habit everybody should develop. Debt is a situation wherein a debtor or borrower owes money to a creditor or lender. In most cases, individuals borrow money from other individuals, payday loan providers, credit card companies, or banks. These loans are usually the subject of contractual agreements which cover how much interest is to be paid and when the money is to be paid back. The interest rate is often dependent on the amount borrowed (known as the principal) and the duration of the loan (known as the time).

Many people decide to borrow money because they feel it is the easiest way out of some situation. While there are sometimes advantages to borrowing money, there are even more disadvantages. Prominent among these is the interest rate, which ensures that the debtor will have to pay more than he or she actually borrowed. It is from this extra amount that the lender makes a profit.

There is also the issue of what happens when a debtor cannot repay the loan on time. This may be disastrous depending on the loan contract. The penalties for default range from increased interest rate to seizure of property. The interest rate may get so high that the borrower is paying so much interest that he is unable to make progress on paying down the principal. This results in situations like an individual who borrowed $5,000 and has paid $15,000 over a two-year period but still owes about $1,500.

In terms of the seizure of properties, most lenders require a pledge of collateral equal in value to the amount borrowed. This may be assets like land, a house, a car, or jewelry. Upon default, the lender may seize the item(s) used as collateral and sell them. Fortunately, the law only allows them to take what they are owed from the proceeds of such sales, so the borrower can recover the balance. However, there is a strong probability that some extra charges will be deducted from this balance, such as the amount spent advertising the seized goods and any other auction costs.

Hence the popular saying: "He who goes a borrowing, goes a sorrowing."

Some lenders are so troublesome that they will give you no rest from the moment you were expected to pay up. They will send representatives, call and send text messages almost every day until you wish you had never borrowed the money in the first place. The pressure could force you into making rash decisions that will cause even more harm.

Imagine a scenario where a man borrows $10,000 to finance a car. His salary is $3,000 per month. He is given a year to pay back the $10,000 along with interest of $2,000, bringing the total to $12,000. He must therefore pay $1,000 on a monthly basis, and by the end of 12 months, his debt will be cleared up.

Considering that his monthly expenses are only about $1,500, that looks very feasible, and he is happy to sign the papers. He makes payments easily until the eighth month, and then he rear-ends another vehicle and gets seriously injured. He will not be able to work for at least two months, so he will not get paid for those two months. His insurance covers some of his medical bills, but he has to pay the rest. The person he collided with is suing him, and he will have to hire a lawyer to help him out. Since he has been paying one-third of his salary on the car loan, he has very little in savings at the moment.

All of this means that he will probably be unable to pay off the car loan on time, and he might also have to enter into new debts to pay for the unexpected expenses. Even if he is able to get back on his feet by the twelfth month and settles every other debt except the initial one for the car, he might end up losing his house just because of that pending debt. This is despite the fact that he had the whole thing well planned out and it looked like nothing could go wrong.

Such scenarios often end up with people trying to find an easy way out. Casinos and online betting are never far away, and many people are tempted to use the little they have left to gamble, hoping to double or triple the money so they can use it to clear their debt. Of course, they not only fail to get the extra money they are looking for; they also end up losing the little they have.

Even worse, the fruitless quest to recover their losses can end up making them addicted to gambling, especially if they got lucky once or twice. If they are eventually able to clear the debt, most of their future earnings – that would once have gone to savings – will go to the casino. The problem with being addicted to gambling is that you lose more than you gain in the long run, in 99.9% of the cases.

A lot of people have gotten their families into unforeseen trouble when they borrowed money they thought they could easily repay but died before they could finish the payments. The assets that their wives and children could have used to start over are instead seized by the creditor.

Even if everything goes as planned, making loan payments makes it almost impossible to set aside money for savings. Interest payments can also be significant. Wouldn't you rather have that money in your savings account?

The bottom line is that if you want to be consistent in saving money, you must develop the habit of staying as far away from debt as possible.

5. Invest Your Money

An excellent money stacking habit to develop is investing your money. When you have the habit of investing your money, you will always be on the lookout for good investments which can generate some passive income. In fact, this is the opposite of going into debt. Instead of collecting capital in the form of a loan and then having to pay back the capital and interest over time, you are paying out capital this time, and you are hoping to get your capital and some interest back in the long run.

Some things in which you can easily invest, with a good chance of profit, are bonds, real estate and stocks. The advantage of investment is that you should make more profit from it than when you just keep your money in a savings account in the bank. You could even make more than your investment if you choose wisely.

Once you've amassed enough capital to make such investments, it will be easier for you to live a comfortable life well within your means and still have more to save and invest. Compare that to living the good life at an earlier time, at the expense of saving and investing – you wouldn't have that option now. Furthermore, your prudent investments can easily serve as a regular source of income after your retirement.

It is true that investments can be very risky. There is a chance that you might lose your principal. However, this shouldn't deter you from investing. Life itself is a risky business. Every night, people go to sleep and never wake up. Does that mean that you shouldn't sleep? The rate of motor vehicle accidents is truly frightening, but we all drive anyway. The same applies to investing. Always try to invest when you can. Just be careful, just like you are careful when you are driving.

One way to do this is to invest in a variety of different stocks and bonds instead of just a particular one. Most of your investments will probably do well, and even if one or two go the wrong way, you should still make a substantial profit in the long run. Another thing you should consider is the use of professionals. There are professional stockbrokers and business analysts you can seek advice from. For a small fee, they will help you find the best stocks to buy and the best time to buy them. If you need to exit your investment, they will be able to advise you on the proper timing to maximize your profit or at least minimize your loss.

You don't need to have a whole lot of money before you start to invest. You can decide to invest $50 every month. If you do this regularly you will have invested $6,000 over the next 10 years, and your profit should be in the same region – or much more. By the time you retire 30 years later, your investment could be bringing you a profit of over $10,000 every month. There are a number of useful investment calculators online if you want to plug in your own numbers.

A very interesting individual when it comes to investing is Warren Buffet. He used to be the second richest person in the world but is currently the fourth richest person in the world and the second richest person in the United States, with a net worth of $73.3 billion as of May 2017. He is probably the most successful investor worldwide. I would have loved to put his story here, but considering the fact that his money stacking habits go well beyond just investments, I will use his story as a case study after explaining some other money stacking habits you should develop. I will also try to identify the major money stacking habits that have helped him to become one of the wealthiest people in the world today.

Investment is very important to having a financially free future. It is therefore key that you should be passionate about investing and invest at every opportunity you have. It is a great way to make money. Most of the people who talk about wealth creation emphasize the need to build a system of making money. This implies that you can make money even while you are sleeping, because you have something working for you that you do not have to be directly involved in.

One such system you can easily build is investing as much as possible. Other people will manage the money you invest to make a profit while you get a share of that profit. Your money will be working for you, while you concentrate on other things that will bring you money. The money flow can continue even after your retirement, and probably even after you are dead. Such investments can easily be willed to family members or even to charity – which brings us to the next point.

6. Dedicate a Certain Percentage of Your Earnings to Philanthropy

Now this is a point that might sound controversial, and one that many people will disagree with. A lot of people will wonder where philanthropy comes in when we are talking about money stacking. Shouldn't we be concentrating on keeping money (saving)? If spending money is unavoidable, shouldn't it be spent on only what we need, as well as on things that will bring us additional money, such as investments?

It is important to note that the world does not revolve around you, and an excellent way to attain happiness is by helping other people. Of course, you might have a number of other things you think could bring you more happiness than giving a percentage of your income to charity. Better still, you could save and invest it, and add it to your wealth.

However, you're surely aware that many wealthy people regularly give some of their money to charity. For example, Bill Gates, who is the richest man in the world, has given several billion dollars to charity. In the year 2000, he founded the Bill and Melinda Gates Foundation, through which he gives huge sums of money for scientific research programs that aim to make the world better for everyone, as well as to different charitable organizations. He also co-founded The Giving Pledge with Warren Buffet. They, alongside other billionaires, have agreed to give a minimum of 50% of their riches to charitable causes. As mentioned earlier, we will be examining Warren Buffet in more details later, and you will also be able to learn more about his philanthropic activities.

Another reason to be a philanthropist is that you will have a mindset of abundance. Giving is linked to receiving, and one school of thought holds that the more you give, the more you receive. Be that as it may, when you are able to give to other people to help them, you will at least get happiness from it.

There are also cases where people have given to others during their time of need and those people have later helped them when their paths crossed again in the future. You could, for example, make regular visits to children at an orphanage. Each of these children has a unique future of his own, and some may grow up to become multi-millionaires. Imagine meeting such a successful kid in the future. He would certainly be willing to do you a favor or two, even if you're still wealthier than he is. Many people have gotten cars, houses, checks, juicy contracts and good jobs for their kids from individuals who have benefitted from their philanthropic activities in the past.

Putting aside three to five percent of your income for charity should not really hurt you, especially considering the happiness you'll get from it now and other gains you might get in the future. One of the greatest investments anybody can ever make is investing in people. This is why people devote so much time and money to raising their children, so that they can grow up with better chances of becoming successful. When you give to charity, you are also investing in people's lives and giving them better chances of becoming successful in the future.

7. Set Up Automatic Payments

People forget things all the time, and with so much on our minds we can forget even the most basic of things. This has led to the saying that the dullest pencil is sharper than the sharpest memory. Writing things down is certainly a good idea, but nowadays, thanks to the advanced computer systems used by banks, things that have to do with payments can easily be automated.

The advantage of this is that you can comfortably forget about monthly bills. You've already taken care of them! You can use the time you save to think about other profitable things to do. You can place standing orders on your account for all your monthly bills, including electricity, water, garbage collection, and rent or mortgage payments. Once this is in place, all these payments will be deducted from your account at the appropriate time. You'll avoid the risk of spending your money on something else and then getting the rude shock that you have not paid a particular monthly bill. Because all your bills will be paid on time, you'll also avoid late charges.

Even without automatic payments, monthly bills are relatively easy to remember – you do get a reminder every month, after all. There's actually a much higher risk of forgetting things like newly incurred bills, pending one-time payments, and yearly fees. Some people can't even remember their own anniversary, so it's no wonder they forget to pay these kinds of bills. Then, of course, they receive a letter informing them that a late fee has been incurred. It is therefore best to set up a payment order the instant you receive a new bill. As long as you have sufficient funds in your account, the money will be paid on time and to the correct party. You should also develop the habit of making yearly fees automatically payable at the particular time of year when they come due.

All you need to do is ensure that the automatic payments are properly set up with your bank. Once the conditions you specify are met, the payments will be made for you. Aside from a certain date, such conditions could include that you have a sufficient amount to cover the payment, that your balance is at least a particular amount, or that you have received your salary for the current month or a particular future month.

Your bank will probably allow you to set up automatic payments to creditors and utility companies. Most banks now offer online banking so that you can easily log into your bank account through the bank's website. This is a convenient way to schedule payments long before they are due – the moment you remember them, or better still, the moment you incur them. This will save you time and effort in the long run, as you will no longer need to write checks or make manual electronic payments every month. That will free up time and energy to work on creating more money and implementing your other money stacking habits. The most important advantage of automatic payments, however, is that you will be saved the expense and frustration of having to pay late fees incurred not because you didn't have the money to pay, but because you forgot the bill was due.

Then too, automatic payments can be a lifesaver if unforeseen circumstances make it impossible for you to pay the bills yourself. Suppose you're hospitalized for three months. Do you want to come home to three months' worth of outstanding bills and late fees? If you have automatic payments set up, you won't have to worry about this as long as you have enough money in your account (or enough coming in from investments) to cover your living expenses for that period. And if you've been money stacking – you will!

8. Develop Yourself

Developing yourself is another money stacking habit that can make you a better saver and enhance your ability to stack even more money. We live our lives based on our abilities. We cannot give what we don't have, and we cannot earn beyond what we have made of ourselves and the value that represents. It is a common saying that knowledge is power. When you know more, you will be able to save more. Once you are able to save more, you will have a higher level of financial independence.

If you really want to boost your money stacking habits, then you must invest some time in reading and learning about finance. You should read books like this one, and if possible you should attend seminars, lectures and even classes on finance. Over time, you will learn what works for you, which strategies you should implement and which of them are not for you. You have to be selective because it would be almost impossible to implement everything you read in every book or hear in every finance class you attend. The more you know, though, the better you will be able to discern the most effective techniques. You'll discover the ones that are right for you, the ones that are wrong, and the ones that are right for some people but wrong for you.

Even if you invest through a professional stockbroker or hire a financial advisor, it is important to know everything that is going on. There are any number of crooked financial advisors who, once they realize that you have no idea of what they are doing with your money, will start helping themselves to your profits. You might only get half – and in some cases much less – of the profit they make with your funds. They will keep the rest for themselves, even as they continue to collect their legitimate charges and fees for managing your account. It is therefore vital that you be knowledgeable about what is happening with your money and the performance of those investments that your money has been put into. A general idea is better than none, but if possible, you should know exactly how much you should receive from each of them.

You should personally read about how to invest your money and how to maximize what you earn on a monthly basis. Subscribe to and read personal finance blogs. The more you know about managing your money, the better you will be able to use it to supplement your salary, and the more you will have for savings.

Apart from developing your financial knowledge, you should also develop your job skills. The type of job you have determines the amount of income you will get. Your income subsequently determines how much you can spend and how much you can save.

There's no way you can save $100 if that's all you make in a month. You'll have to pay bills and buy food, after all. No matter how disciplined you are financially, there is no way you will be able to save more than $20 to $30 a month if your overall monthly income is $100.

However, if you develop your skills, your monthly income might rise to $200. That would make it much easier to save $100. If you were able to manage on $70 to $80 a month in the past, investing the remaining $20 to $30 (or at least some of it) toward developing yourself in your field would have been an excellent investment, right?

There are many ways to develop yourself, depending on your current level of knowledge and experience. Most employers pay according to how skilled you are and the degrees and professional certifications you have. Here are some ways to develop yourself in order to increase your earning power:

On the job training: If you are a waiter, truck driver, salesperson, secretary, farmhand or cashier, you can easily train yourself as you work. Be conscious of how things are done, observing more experienced coworkers and learning from them. Listen to instructions from your supervisor, and find out what qualifications and certifications he has. If you do this conscientiously for some time, you will notice that you have improved a lot – and so will the management. Your superiors will commend you, and when the time comes they will promote or give you a raise. You will also have the opportunity to look for better paying jobs in bigger organizations.

If you have the time, you could attend night school or take online classes to get the qualifications that would let you become a supervisor. If you save regularly, you might eventually have enough money to start your own business in the same field, thereby becoming an employer of labor and earning even more.

Apprenticeship: Welders, HVAC technicians, plumbers, mechanics, masons, electricians, carpenters and the like learn their trade as apprentices. This presents an opportunity. For example, suppose you have been working for a small-time plumber, fixing minor residential plumbing problems. You can save enough money to last you for a few months, then quit and get an apprenticeship in a larger company which handles the plumbing for commercial buildings. If your apprenticeship goes well, the company is likely to hire you when it is complete. At the very least, you'll have a better chance of getting a job with another major plumbing company, with a bigger paycheck. If you'd just stayed with the smaller plumber without improving yourself, you wouldn't have that opportunity.

Vocational certification: As a paralegal, dental assistant, cosmetologist or chef, you can improve your chances of getting a higher paying job by getting a vocational certification. This could be a diploma from an institute in your field or from a university. Such a qualification will allow you to work in more reputable institutions – 5-star hotels and restaurants if you're a chef, for example – with correspondingly better pay. Working at such places will also offer better experience and more regular promotions.

Associate Degree: As a licensed practical nurse, draftsman or commercial artist, you might want to get an associate degree. With your degree, you will be able to apply for jobs in bigger institutions with higher entry standards – and higher paychecks. You will also have a better chance of attracting high profile clients if you decide to become a self-employed consultant in your field.

Higher Apprenticeship: As a lawyer, management consultant, chartered accountant or chartered engineer, you have the opportunity to do a higher apprenticeship with your current employer. This experience will supplement your educational qualifications and make you more attractive to bigger companies with better remuneration packages and perks such as travel allowances and all-expense-paid vacations.

Undergraduate Degree: As a software developer, registered nurse, teacher or accountant, you can enroll in a university or college for an undergraduate degree. Having a degree will increase your market value and your chances of getting a good job with a higher paycheck.

Professional Degree: As a medical doctor, lawyer, engineer, dentist or architect, you can consider getting a professional degree to further boost your value. This is a sure way to get a raise while remaining with your current employer, as your salary will automatically be upgraded to match what those with similar degrees are being paid.

Graduate Degree: As a university professor, scientist, nurse practitioner or mathematician, you could take a graduate degree. As with a professional degree, this will inevitably boost your paycheck, and it could lead to a promotion as well.

No matter what your line of work, there are always chances for improving yourself and securing a better remuneration package. When you do, the amount you're able to stack as you save towards projects, emergencies and retirement will increase substantially.

9. Learn to Monetize Unused Household Items

As our lives change, so do our needs, which means that we tend to accumulate items that are no longer useful. For instance, you might have bought a laptop with adequate specifications for photo editing but then gotten into video editing. Since video editing requires more processing power, you now need to buy a better laptop. Well, don't just let the first laptop sit around the house gathering dust; once you get the new one, sell the old one for some extra cash.

There are many advantages to selling off items you no longer you require at home (or at work, if you're a business owner). First of all, the item continues to depreciate even if you're no longer using it. If you don't use that laptop for a couple of years, the battery will be dead, and you'll need to get a new one before you can sell it for full price. The model of the laptop will be less modern as well. If this particular model was released four years before you stopped using it, after two more years, it will be six years away from being current. Anybody would pay more for a four-year-old laptop than a six-year-old one whose technology might be nearly obsolete. Finding a buyer at all will be difficult, as most people will be aiming to buy something with a newer processor. You'd probably be lucky to get 10% of what you paid for it.

This is especially relevant for high-tech electronics such as computers and cell phones, but it applies to virtually everything else, too. If you sell items the instant you have no more use for them, you will be able to get more money from them. You can channel this money into your savings account, and it can come in handy in the future when you have to upgrade your equipment yet again.

There are a number of easy ways to monetize items you are no longer using. Ask family and friends if they are interested in the item or know anyone who might be. Then you just have to agree on a price. Another option is to take it somewhere used items are sold, such as a pawn shop. They'll buy it from you and sell it on at a profit.

If the item is damaged, take it to a junkyard or repair shop. They may want it for spare parts, or they may want to refurbish it and sell it themselves. You can do this with old laptops, phones, televisions, bikes and cars, as well as various other items.

There are many internet marketplaces for buying and selling used items. You can register on such a website and advertise the product you want to sell with a price and a detailed description. Within a short time, an interested buyer will contact you to negotiate on the price, payment method, and delivery terms. If you live nearby you can meet in person; otherwise, he might make a transfer to your bank account while you ship the product to him. The most popular websites for selling used items are Craigslist and eBay.

If you have exercise equipment, furniture or other large items to sell, you can hold a yard sale.

Monetization of items gives you the opportunity to make money from things that you no longer need or that are no longer functioning. You will end up with some extra funds you can put in your savings account.

Another advantage to selling off the things you don't need is that you will have a neater, more organized home. This in itself could be a very big bonus to your money stacking goals. When you have too many unused items in your room, the room could become so cluttered that it's difficult to move around. You could trip over something you're not using and fall on and destroy something you actually need! Then you'll have to pull money from your savings to repair or replace it.

When you're reviewing what to get rid of, the major suspects include books you've already read, DVDs you've already watched, CDs you've gotten sick of listening to, toys your children have outgrown, gadgets that have become obsolete and clothes that have gone out of style. If you're worried about selling an item you might still need in the future, you might carry out a check on your house every two months. If you see anything that you have not used for the past two months, sell it and put the money in your savings account.

10. Avoid Eating Out

Eating out is a major expense for many people, especially bachelors and bachelorettes whose social lives are so busy that they do not have time to go grocery shopping, let alone actually cook. So they spend money every day on lunch from a fast food restaurant and dinner from a Chinese takeout.

Apart from the fact that these foods aren't very healthy, they cost more than cooking at home. It's much better to pack your lunch and cook your dinners yourself. If you're too busy to cook every night, you might consider cooking more when you do have time and then eating the leftovers for the next several days. You can use the weekend for grocery shopping, making sure you get enough to last you all through the week. Once this is taken care of, you can cook in the evenings, eat a hot dinner, and use the leftovers for lunch the following day.

You can easily save more than $2,000 a year when you prepare your own lunches. If you've been eating both lunch and dinner out, that would be over $4,000 saved by cooking at home. This is a significant sum to add to your emergency fund or savings account!

Another benefit to cooking at home is that you can use the ingredients you love and are comfortable with to make healthy, fresh meals. Being conscious of your health every time you cook will also encourage you to carry out other fitness activities that will boost your health. This will allow you to save money that would have gone to doctors and medications.

Many people argue that it is faster to eat out. The fact is that this might not always be true. First, you have to travel to a restaurant, which can take over an hour each way. Apart from the amount you spend on the food, you have to pay for gas or public transportation. Then you'll have to wait for them to take your order and serve your food. This could be as little as two minutes at a fast food joint, but for a sit-down place it's going to be more like 20 or 30.

The fact is that you can cook your own meal in 20 to 30 minutes if you've planned properly. With a freezer and microwave, you can even cook for the whole week ahead on the weekend. All you have to do on workdays is take the food from the freezer and microwave it for a few minutes. You can take the same food to work as lunch. Coffee and toast could do for breakfast; that doesn't take too much time.

So apart from saving money and living healthier, you'll probably be saving time as well when you eat at home. Cooking for yourself and avoiding restaurants is a great help in reaching your money stacking goals.

11. Research things you need to buy

Research is obviously very important in the invention of new technologies, but it is not limited to this. At the personal level, our parents researched the foods they gave us, the clothes they bought for us, and the schools they sent us to. As we grew up, we also did some research before settling on a profession to pursue and a university to attend. Too often, however, we neglect the need to carry out research on prices before buying things. Considering the fact that this could be a continuous money saving advantage, many people are losing a fortune by not conducting research before making purchases. They are a number of reasons why you should conduct research before you buy absolutely anything.

First, you should conduct research to learn about the type of item you're planning to buy. What are the different brands? Which of the brands are overpriced because they're targeted towards the rich and those who love to show off? Which of the brands offer the best quality? Which of the brands have good customer support and convenient repair centers? Which of the brands have the best warranties, and which actually honor them without a hassle? Which of the brands make the most durable products? Which of the brands have spare parts readily available?

Spending a few minutes to get the answers to all of these questions will guide you toward buying the right product.

If you want to buy a television, for example, you might be tempted to go for a Samsung. It's a very popular brand, and they are great in terms of most of these questions. However, their pricing is generally high. LG is competitive with Samsung in all of the other areas, and their prices are often a bit cheaper.

The same applies to lesser known domestic brands. They'll be cheaper than the big names, and if they have a factory or service center in your city, produce a durable product, and give a good warranty, why not go with them?

On the other hand, consider what might happen if you buy an imported TV just because it's cheap. If something goes wrong with it, you might not be able to find a repair center that can fix it, or the repair center might not be able to find the requisite spare parts. In that case, you'll be forced to buy a new TV, and you probably won't even be able to sell the old one as scrap. You'll end up having spent more money than if you'd bought an expensive brand to begin with.

Once you have shortlisted some promising brands, ones with positive answers to all the questions above, you can now consider pricing. You should be buying the best item, based on your research, whose price is within your budget. When you have narrowed it down to that one item, compare prices for it in different stores, as they could vary slightly. In the end, you should get it from a reputable store with the cheapest price, after confirming that everything is in order. Be especially careful to ensure that the item is not counterfeit and is covered by the manufacturer's warranty.

Speaking further about price, you might also want to look for stores or websites where you can get discounts, gift cards, codes or coupons for the product. Sometimes this can substantially reduce how much you pay for the product. With a 5%-off coupon, you can get a $500 discount on a car worth $10,000. You can also look for people who have gift cards for the item but do not need it; they will probably be willing to sell you the card for less than face value.

Finally, remember that you'll often pay less if you can wait a while. Usually the price for a newly-released item will be relatively high. Within a few weeks, though, the product may be selling for a mere fraction of its original price.

12. Be Accountable to Someone

Another money stacking habit you should develop is finding someone you can be accountable to. When you are accountable to someone you respect, or someone who can warn you about questionable spending, you will be more careful with how you spend money, and you will always be able to get a second opinion on what's appropriate. You won't spend $100 of your $700 salary buying chocolates if you know you'd have to tell your husband about it.

A partner you are accountable to, who is also aware that you are developing money stacking habits, can help you get used to these habits. His corrections – and even thinking about what he would tell you – could stop you from making silly mistakes with your spending and not staying true to these habits you are developing.

If you are married, it's easiest to make your spouse your accountability partner. This will work best if this partner also understands the importance of money stacking habits and is practicing them himself. In this case, you can each act as the accountability partner for the other. It's always easier to tell when someone else is making a mistake than when you're making one. That's why everyone seems to be a good adviser but most people aren't nearly as good at making the best decisions for themselves.

Otherwise, you can use a disciplined close and trusted friend or family member who understands the principles of wealth and the importance of abiding by them. You can also enlighten the partner on the exact money stacking habits you are developing, which will give him a basis for assessing you and correcting you when you go wrong. He might even suggest additional habits to develop.

If you don't have a suitable family member or friend, you can hire a financial advisor. While this will cost you some money, it will be well worth it. The advisor might even be more frank and strict with you than a family member or friend, who might sometimes cut you some slack because they don't want to offend you or get into an argument.

You might also tend to respect the views and opinions of a financial expert more than those of a family member or friend. You just have to ensure that you find a reputable advisor, with track record of helping people save and invest money in profitable manner, and you should be fine.

When you are aware that someone is paying attention to the things you buy and the way you live, you will tend to be more careful about honoring your promises and abiding by your money stacking habits. You will not want your accountability partner to be disappointed in you or give up on you. Apart from a financial advisor, the best accountability partner is a family member or friend who is just as eager to change his habits and save money – or better still, someone who has already mastered money stacking habits and is already benefitting from them.

13. Learn How to Make Use of Your Time

There is a very common saying that time is money. The way we use our time determines how much money we have.

Many people love to get to a place called the comfort zone. They have a nine-to-five job, a house, a car, and they can comfortably get by every month with what they earn. They can comfortably take care of their needs, and their most important wants, without getting into debt. If they have an emergency, they have a healthy credit limit they can use to survive it, and they can easily pay off the debt in a few months just by cutting down on some luxuries.

However, they do not have substantial savings, nor are they really considering accumulating some savings for the future. They expect to work till they are 65 and then live off of social security. They are therefore not even thinking of doing anything profitable with their free time.

It is important to note that both the rich and the poor have 24 hours in a day. The difference is that the rich, who don't have to work two or three jobs just to survive, have more free time to devote to making more money. Being rich is partly a matter of having rich parents and better opportunities, but there is also an element of effort and hard work. Someone who's born rich but doesn't make good use of his time may not stay rich – and someone who's born poor but strives for success every minute of the day may, with luck, make it to the top.

If you don't start out rich, it will be impossible to get that way without working hard, developing yourself, and adopting money stacking habits. Even if someone wins $10 million in the lottery, if he doesn't have saving habits and investment sense, he'll have spent it all and be back to square one within a couple of years. In the first year, he'll buy everything he ever wanted, starting with expensive (and expensive to maintain) sports cars and multi-million-dollar mansions that come with sky-high property taxes and huge staffing requirements. That will exhaust the $10 million. In the second year, he'll be selling the cars and the mansions and laying off the staff. Eventually he'll be forced to sell the last car and last mansion, and that will be that.

People who want to be wealthy don't depend on luck. They understand that they must make a deliberate effort to use their time correctly. Suppose a person with money stacking habits and a person without money stacking habits both have $100 left with them 10 days before the end of the month. They will have very different mindsets regarding how to spend the money.

The one with the money stacking habits will be imagining how much more he can earn before the end of the month, and will use his free time to try to get it. He will plan to work for an extra two hours every day for the next 10 days, making $10 per day and spending $5 per day, thereby saving an extra $50 to add to the initial $100.

The other person, without money stacking habits, will be thinking of how to spend the $100 so that it will last him for the remaining 10 days. By the time it's gone, he'll get his next paycheck, so why worry? He will therefore budget $10 for each day. In most cases, however, such an individual won't be able to stick to his plan. By the fifth day, he might have spent $80 already and have only $20 left. He might revise his budget to spend $4 per day for the remaining five days but end up exhausting the $20 in two days. To tide him over for the remaining three days, he might borrow $25 or $50. When he finally gets his paycheck, he'll have to pay off the loan.

If you have a regular nine-to-five job, using an extra two hours to work every other day, plus four hours on Saturday, should not be a big deal. It helps if you have a skill that you can use for part-time jobs during this time. For example, you could learn how to play a musical instrument and join a band that performs at evening or weekend events. You could learn photography and take pictures of birthdays and weddings. If you are more of an introvert, you might consider freelance activities like website design, logos and other graphic designs, or writing articles and e-books. All of these are great ways of earning some extra income in just a few hours a week. Once your part-time job starts bringing you regular income, you might decide to use that to pay your expenses for the month while putting the salary from your day job into your savings.

14. Portray Yourself Modestly

A major component of living beyond one's means is 'keeping up with the Joneses', i.e., trying to show everybody how rich you are by buying expensive things like solid gold wristwatches, diamond necklaces, and the latest iPhone. The competition is often very fierce, because new gadgets and items are released every day. If it's not a phone, it's a designer jacket, or a $10,000 limited edition pair of basketball shoes.

Some people feel that they immediately have to buy these items and wear them so that everybody knows that they can afford the most expensive things. They get into a huge amount of debt doing this, and sometimes even turn to criminalities like embezzlement just to raise the money to keep up. Of course, they can never get everything they want. They are often sad and frustrated individuals hiding behind smiling faces that show a happiness just as fake as their lifestyles. Eventually their crimes catch up with them, and they end up on the street or in prison.

Don't let that happen to you! Portraying yourself modestly should be one of your money stacking habits. When people around you know that you are modest, they will not expect you to try to impress them. They will also tend to respect you more.

Drawing less attention to yourself helps in two ways. On the one hand, your friends and family members won't see you as a multi-millionaire who can afford $10,000 shoes and should therefore be able to help them out with $50 whenever they're short. If you are wearing those shoes, they'll never believe you don't have the cash. You might have to hand over your last dime just to save face when you get hit up by a family member or very close friend to whom you can't say no. A modest person, on the other hand, can credibly say he doesn't have the money to give, or can give only what he can actually afford.

Expensive possessions also attract criminals. Some petty thieves might be satisfied with snatching your iPhone 7 or robbing you of your golden wristwatch at knifepoint. They'll be satisfied getting a quick $1,000 from the fence, even if the actual value is over $20,000. If you're less fortunate, you may fall afoul of professionals who will kidnap you for ransom. Their (not unreasonable) theory is that if you're stepping out wearing $20,000 worth of accessories, you probably have access to $100,000 for the ransom.

Living modestly is therefore a good idea for reasons that extend far beyond the money you'll save.

15. Don't Gamble

Gambling is a great way to stack money – for casinos, racetracks and bookies. You, on the other hand, should stay well away from it.

It's an understandable temptation. Who wouldn't love to use $100 today to win $1,000,000 tomorrow? In fact, anybody in their right mind would be willing to use $1,000 today to win $1,100 tomorrow. This is what gambling promises to everybody, even though the reality is that only one in a hundred thousand people will ever win $1,000,000 on a $100 bet. And 99% of those lucky few will be right back to where they started – or even worse off – in five years. That's because they'll have put $100,000 into leading a louche lifestyle and the remaining $900,000 back into gambling, with no results to show for it.

A major problem with gambling is that it's addictive. It doesn't matter if the gambler is winning or losing. If he's winning, he'll see the activity as profitable and will continue to invest in it. When he starts to lose, he'll keep playing to try to win his money back. Eventually he'll lose everything he made from gambling – and everything he ever made doing anything else. Gambling ends up ruining almost everybody who tries it. It becomes a habit that results in loss of faith, self-respect, dignity, friendships and property, and leads to debt, embarrassment, suffering and pain.

David Milch is an example of a person who lost everything he ever earned to gambling. A screenwriter who was formerly an English literature professor at Yale, he is obviously extremely talented. Known for his unorthodox and cerebral approach to writing, he won the Emmy award four times and is a co-creator of both Deadwood and NYPD Blue. Unfortunately, he also had a severe gambling problem. A lawsuit filed against him in 2015 alleged that he gambled away $25 million between 2000 and 2011. Although he had a stellar 30-year career in Hollywood, during which he made over $100 million, the lawsuit indicated that he owed the IRS $17 million and was living on just $40 a week.

Well, maybe Milch just wasn't a very good gambler, you say. And it's true that some people have made their fortune in gambling.

And then lost it the same way.

Consider Stu Ungar. At one point he had over $1 million he made from gambling during the 80s. He promptly went on a two-month losing streak, lost everything, got hooked on cocaine, and ended up dying alone and penniless at the age of 45.

Still not convinced? Between 1993 and 1995, Archie Karas amassed a fortune of $40 million dollars from gambling. He lost it all on craps and was later caught with marked cards at a California blackjack table, raising speculations that he might have been cheating all along.

These are just two of the many people who made fortunes from gambling and ended up worse off than they started. Gambling will not only take away the money you would have saved; it will also take all the money you would have used for living expenses, and then it will take your car and your house.

16. Bulk Purchasing

Bulk purchasing is another habit you should develop. For items that you always need and that don't expire quickly, buy them in bulk if it will save you money. If a 5-pound bag of flour goes for $3 while a 25-pound sack of the same flour goes for $8, get the larger size. If you use five pounds of flour every month, at the end of five months, you'll have saved $7 just by buying in bulk.

Sometimes you see 'buy 2, get 1 free' deals. If you'll finish using all three items before their expiration date, then by all means go for it. You save 33.3 per cent off the total cost. If you can buy copies of your favorite magazine at the newsstand for $5 but a yearly subscription is $50, go ahead and subscribe.

If you use Questia Online Library, their quarterly subscription is $49.99, while their yearly subscription is $99.99. If you are a student or lecturer and you know you will be subscribing all year, instead of paying a total of $199.96 for quarterly subscriptions, get a one-year subscription and save almost 50% at $99.97.

There are so many opportunities to save a substantial amount of money by buying things in bulk when you know you will buy them eventually anyway.

17. Save Windfall Income

Sometimes we're lucky enough to get some money that we weren't expecting. For instance, if you work as a computer engineer for a salary of $5,000 a month, all your expenses will be planned around that amount. Now imagine that you're lazing around the house one weekend and you suddenly receive a call from somebody who needs an IT system set up by Monday. He offers you $1,000, and you readily agree to help him out.

Now, what will you do with that money? Instead of immediately blowing it on your favorite vice, you could decide to save it. That way it will become part of your emergency fund. Even if you eventually decide to spend the money, you will have gotten some time to really think about what you should use it for. You'll end up getting something valuable and necessary instead of just a temporary thrill that would only have distracted you and taken time away from your personal development.

18. Be Frugal with Your Spending

The reason why many people who have good paying jobs end up working for years without building up any savings is that they are not frugal in their spending. They are always on the lookout for the latest fashion accessories and gadgets, and they end up spending all their money on flashy things. Once there is any little setback, they immediately find themselves living on credit.

Being frugal with your money lets you have the most important things you need to buy and still save money. Instead of buying expensive brands of what you need, you simply go for cheaper brands that still produce quality products. For instance, why would you want to buy a $1,000 wristwatch when you can get a perfectly good one for $10? You'll still know what time it is. Don't buy a luxury car (which will also have higher fuel consumption and very expensive spare parts); just get a basic model that's durable and has good fuel efficiency as well as available and affordable spare parts.

Do this and you'll be spending less on buying things and less on maintaining them. You will also draw less attention (especially from thieves). Being mugged because you are wearing a $1,000 watch is a real possibility. A person wearing a cheap wristwatch will hardly attract that type of attention, and even if he is robbed, he'll lose a lot less.

When you want to buy any item, avoid the very top brands, those whose brand names are even more expensive than their products. If the top brand costs $500 but the item is only worth $100, you know that the brand name is the reason for the extra $400. Going for a lesser known brand will get you essentially the same item for the $100 that it's worth, so you will get the full value from your money. Whether you want to buy a car, clothes, shoes, a phone – whatever – you should place more emphasis on the value and quality of the item than the brand.

19. Save Your Loose Change

Many people use their loose change to get items they don't really need, or even want. For instance, some people, when they find themselves with a few loose cents, end up buying candy. It's not because they really want candy; it's just that they can't think of anything better to do with the money. When you find yourself with coins in your pocket, don't just get whatever they'll buy you – save them!

You don't have to go to the bank every time you have a little loose change to deposit. You can just get a piggy bank. Anytime you have any loose change, put it in the piggy bank. Whenever it gets full, take it to the bank and add it to your savings account. You will be very surprised at how much you find in your piggy bank whenever you go to check.

If you have certain items you want to buy for your house, you can designate such savings for them. You might also want to use this money for emergency repairs that might come up, say fixing cracked pipes or painting walls. That way you won't need to go and draw money from your main savings or use your credit to pay for such expenses.

20. Use Coupons and Gift Cards

The use of coupons and gift cards will help you in your quest to save money. A coupon is an electronic or paper document that can be redeemed for a discount when buying a particular product or service. They are usually given by retailers or manufacturers to customers to promote sales. They often come with an expiration date. An example would be a coupon that gives you 20 per cent off when you buy goods worth over $100.

A gift card can be electronic or plastic. (There is a paper version, often called a voucher.) It usually has a specific value. It can be used to pay for products and services. Some gift cards expire, while others do not. It is possible to get gift cards from banks, groups of retailers, or individual retailers.

If you have a $10 gift card, you can use it to buy goods worth $10 from a specific store or stores. If you want to buy goods worth $60, you can pay $50 in cash alongside the $10 gift card. It is possible to combine more than one gift card to make a purchase.

A great way to save money is to visit stores where you are given gift cards and coupons for regular patronage or purchases over a certain amount. All you need to do is keep the coupon or gift card in a safe place and take it along with you on your next visit to the store (making sure that is before any expiration date). When you have a coupon that gives you a certain percentage off, you might want to use it to purchase as many big-ticket items as possible to maximize your savings. Of course, you also have to resist the temptation of buying things you don't really need just because you want to get more of a discount from the coupon.

Whenever the opportunity arises, always try to collect and use coupons and gift cards. The money you save by using them can be saved for future use.

21. Compare Prices before Making Purchases

Just as there are different brands that sell the same items for different prices, there are also different stores that sell exactly the same brand and model of an item for different prices. In this case, you will be getting exactly the same thing for a higher or lower price just because you are buying it from a particular store. In order to avoid paying more than you have to for a particular item, compare the prices in different stores before you decide where to buy. Just make sure that the item you're buying isn't cheaper because it's been damaged or something like that.

22. Automatically Deduct Your Savings

Once you're earning enough that you can comfortably save, you should decide how much you want to be saving every month. This amount should then be put on automatic payment so that it is sent to a different account, preferably a dedicated savings account. This will limit the access you have to these funds and ensure that you're not tempted to find an excuse to spend them. You can also have a different account for your emergency fund, which you will have access to, but for which you might not have a card or online banking facility. With a card linked to the account, or activated online banking, it would be too easy to spend the money on situations that aren't really emergencies. With an isolated account that you don't have easy access to, you'll have to go down to the bank and get the money in person, and you're only likely to do that when it's extremely important.

Just like the automatic payments that you've set up for your monthly bills, you should have a standing order for the percentage of your income you intend to save every month. If you are bent on saving 20% of your total income, you will have to make a conscious effort to deposit any income you receive in the form of cash (maybe from your part-time jobs or gifts) to your account. This will allow the 20% to be removed to your savings before you start to spend it. It will thus become a routine that 20% of all the money you earn is to be saved.

If your total monthly income is $1,000 and you intend to save 20%, just pretend that you are earning only $800. You will still survive on that amount. It's as if the other $200 doesn't even exist, because it goes directly to your savings account as your retirement savings. Since the remaining $800 is your total income, you must deduct savings for emergencies and major purchases from it. You might spend $500 and put $300 aside toward your dreams of buying a car and building a house, as well as emergencies such as replacing broken appliances and making household repairs.

Once you've made money stacking habits an integral part of your life, you will be surprised at how easy and how satisfying it can be to save money. When you look at your savings account balance and see that you have saved over $10,000 in just five months by saving your salary of $2,000 while living within the $600 you make doing part-time jobs during your spare time, you'll jump for joy!

23. Maintain Your Equipment Properly

There is a common saying that a stitch in time saves nine. The implication is that when you address a problem the instant something starts to go bad, you will be saving yourself a lot of stress of effort in the future. To put it in dollar terms, what would cost you a dollar to fix now might end up costing you $9 later.

We use many items every day, so it's inevitable that they will start to get worn out and need some maintenance. Unfortunately, many people – out of carelessness or laziness – allow things to degrade so badly that they essentially become irreparable, and possibly dangerous. For instance, a leaky tire could be patched for a few dollars; if it's not, it could lead to a serious accident resulting in car repair bills in the best case and funeral costs in the worst. Something as simple as failing to ensure there is enough water in your car's radiator could cause the engine to burn up. Your insurance company will argue that the damage is due to your carelessness, so they won't pay. Unless you want to fight them in court (where you'd probably lose), you'll have to buy a new engine yourself.

Another place where a stitch in time can save nine is in a building. Not properly maintaining a building, for example by failing to fix cracks in walls, can result in the collapse of the structure and the destruction of all who dwell within it. Many people have lost their lives in building collapses for want of maintenance that would have cost a few hundred dollars at the most. Even if nobody dies, the amount spent rebuilding the house and replacing the furniture will be orders of magnitude greater than the small amount it would have cost to repair the cracks.

Speaking of furniture, it should be regularly checked and glued, nailed or screwed as necessary to avoid sudden decomposition and the necessity to repurchase. Any sparking wires should be checked by an electrician before they cause a fire that consumes the building. The garage door opener should be regularly checked and a technician summoned as soon as any issue is noticed. Otherwise it may suddenly slam down on the car while you're driving under it, killing or seriously injuring you. Your doors should be checked to ensure that they aren't likely to fall on somebody or spontaneously break in two. Gas cylinders should be check for leaks and either fixed or replaced to avoid the risk of an explosion that could blow you to kingdom come the next time you're trying to cook dinner. (Gas cylinders should preferably be kept outside, but that doesn't mean they shouldn't be checked for leaks. A smoker passing by a leaking cylinder could still lead to the house getting burnt down.) Always keep explosives away from ignition sources. Heed warnings in instruction manuals, and do not use electrical equipment of the wrong voltage. Never expose photosensitive materials to direct sunlight.

Maintenance is extremely important, not only in keeping you and your family safe, but also to ensure that you spend as little as possible keeping your electronics and other items working at optimal capacity. There's no point leaving them until they are spoiled beyond repair or a major component will have to be replaced at exorbitant prices.

24. Avoid Cigarettes and Alcohol

Cigarettes and alcoholic beverages are a major money burner for a lot of people even before considering the health risks that they pose.

Cigarettes are perhaps the only product that is sold with a warning that those who use it as intended are liable to die young. Other products come with warnings, of course, but these warnings cover situations in which the product is used incorrectly. Cigarettes, on the other hand, are sold to be smoked, and it is written right on the package that smoking will kill you. Most people start smoking because of peer pressure and maybe the false promise that it helps to relieve stress. What they don't realize is that most of the people they see smoking, including their favorite celebrities, are probably trying to quit. Unfortunately, once someone is addicted to smoking, it is almost impossible for them to stop. That's why it's better to smoke your first cigarette: after the first one, if you decide you want to smoke your last one, you might never be able to.

Countless people die from lung cancer and other diseases caused directly as a result of smoking. Before they do, they spend a huge amount on cigarettes. Some people spend as much as $50 every month. After 10 years of that they will have spent $6,000 just for cigarettes. If they try to quit, they may spend more money on therapy, which could be as much as $5,000 in some cases. And there isn't even any guarantee that the therapy will be effective. Many people have had to spend thousands of dollars for medical treatment and still ended up dead. Those who survive have depleted their savings and gotten into debt. They have to start from square one financially, even while they are still trying to recover from their health problems.

Alcohol is another vice that makes it impossible for some people to save anything. Any money that would have gone to their savings goes to liquor instead. They may go on regular drinking sprees with their friends, spending as much as $100 at a sitting. (When it comes to liquid, it's only alcohol that's consumed in such quantities. Give the same person a bottle of water and he might not even finish it!)

Alcohol is also not without its health dangers, as the liver and kidney may become overworked as they try to rid the body of the toxic substances in alcohol. Many alcoholics spend years on dialysis before finally having to buy a new kidney and pay for transplant surgery. They end up with one kidney, and despite that, they still find it difficult to give up alcohol.

Another way alcohol can rob people of their savings is with assistance of the police. It is against the law in the United States, and in most other countries, to drive after drinking. Slogans like 'if you must drink, don't drive' are commonly used to inform people of this. However, this does not seem to be strong enough to deter hardcore drinkers. Many drunkards will drive themselves to their favorite bar and then try to drive themselves back home at the end of the night. Of course, any halfway vigilant policeman can easily tell that they are driving under the influence of alcohol. They are stopped, given tickets, and sometimes detained. Not only will they have to pay the fine, but they might also go to jail and lose the income they would have made working.

A significant percentage of traffic accidents are the fault of drunk drivers. Alcohol in the bloodstream usually leads to erratic behavior. When a person is driving drunk, he is at heightened risk of being involved in an accident. The risk of being disabled and not being able to work should be enough reason for anybody to stay away from alcohol. Overall, alcohol is an expensive habit that involves the risk of serious health problems, injury, disability and death, as well as incarceration and loss of or damage to your vehicle.

25. Check Your Credit Report for Errors

Another habit you should develop to further your goal of saving money is to check your credit report for errors. There are instances where you might be charged double for an item you purchased. Perhaps you paid at a POS terminal and the money was deducted from your account, but the receipt was not printed out. It will look like an incomplete transaction, and the process will be repeated, resulting in double charges. Furthermore, there are the issues of fraud and identity theft, either by bank employees or hackers. For many online transactions, a hacker does not necessarily need to have your PIN to loot your account. The details written on your credit card are sufficient.

At the end of every month, or at least every quarter, you should request a copy of your credit report and read through it thoroughly to be sure you haven't been double charged and that there are no transactions on the report of which you are unaware. If you notice any sign of a problem, you should immediately forward a complaint to your bank through your personal banker or customer service representative. They will be able to investigate the complaint and help you recover your money.

Do not expose your bank cards to anybody, no matter how close they are to you. The only exception would be if you have a joint account with your spouse. You should also register for text and e-mail alerts so that you receive notification immediately whenever there is a credit or debit to your account. It will be easier to cancel unauthorized charges if you contact the bank right after the transaction occurs.

Money not lost to double charges or fraud is money that you can use to pay your bills and save.

Steps to Building Habits

New habits are not built overnight. It is also generally more difficult to build good habits than bad habits. While bad habits are often pleasurable, good habits can be very difficult and require a lot of sacrifice. You have to make a conscious effort to build good habits, including money stacking habits.

The first thing you will need to do while building a new good habit is to focus on the habit. It is easy to get carried away by some short-term pleasure and forget about the habit you are trying to develop. You should therefore choose a good location and time to make it an everyday (or at least every weekday) activity. Say early in the morning, at the gym, during lunch break, while traveling, the instant you get to the office (you might want to get to the office a bit earlier in this case, to avoid distractions and so that you don't eat into your working time), after the close of work in the office (this could also be used to make up for days you got to the office late) or during the evenings in your house. All of these are great times to focus on the new habit you are building. At first, this will help to warn you when you are about to take any action that counters the habit; later, once the habit has truly become a part of you, such actions will no longer cross your mind.

The next thing you should do is to pick one routine at time. When you try to do everything at once, your willpower will be relatively weak, and you might just give up. Or you may not be able to remember all of your goals at once, leading to poor results and frustration. Pick one habit and give yourself a month to master it. If possible, break the habits into four different aspects and take a week to master each one. The simpler and easier the habit seems, the better things will go.

Don't expect a perfect result on the first day, or even the tenth day. There will be times when the urge to do something against the habit will be so strong that you won't be able to resist it. Or you might do something before you remember that it is one of the things you are trying to build a habit against. When that happens, do not give up. Continue with the process of building the habit. Know that such failures are normal at that beginning stage, but do not use that as an excuse to always break the habit you are developing. That would only make it more difficult and you would require a longer time to achieve the habit.

Have a checklist of logical actions that you should carry out to achieve the habit. Money stacking habits are logical, and you can break each one down into a set of logical actions. For instance, not to be indebted implies actions such as paying off every existing debt; ensuring that expenses are well outlined and budgeted for; ensuring that things not budgeted for are not bought or are shifted forward to the next month; using your emergency fund only for extremely urgent matters; etc.

Some of the reasons why you should adopt money stacking habits have been listed above. You can look for more reasons, preferably personal reasons, why you must always have a substantial amount of money in your savings account. It could be that you want to start your own business, or you want to retire early and spend more time with your family, or that you have experienced being completely broke and it was not a pleasant experience. This reason or reasons will serve as motivation to keep you going whenever you get discouraged and start to wonder why you can't just eat lunch out for the next week instead of cooking this weekend, or why you can't just go on a shopping spree in Dubai.

You will also have to be accountable not only to yourself but to someone else who can check on you. You should always take the time to reflect on your progress in your money stacking habits and evaluate whether you are getting the results you were hoping for. There should never be an indication that you are saving less, depleting your savings account (except if there has been a major emergency), or treading water for a significant period of time (no addition or subtraction to your savings for several months). Comparing how much you have in your savings account on a monthly basis, and determining the reasons for any unexpected changes, is a great way to measure your progress in the spirit of being accountable.

Motivation is always key to developing habits. In addition to keeping in mind the reason why you are developing the money stacking habit, you should also occasionally reward yourself with small but enjoyable treats. For every $10,500 you have saved, you might want to use $500 to treat yourself to a delicious lunch. Or you could add this money to your budget for the month so that you can get some things you've wanted but have been denying yourself. You might want to give yourself some free time and spend the weekend watching movies and playing football instead of going to your part-time job.

You should also make sure you repeat the habits continuously, as many times as possible, till they become so much a part of you that you can easily overcome any temptation to indulge in an activity that goes against your habit.

Considering the fact that there are sure to be challenges and disruptions at the beginning stage, you should have an if-then plan. In a scenario where you wanted to save $100 for the month but only ended up saving $90, you can move the $10 forward and try to save it from next month's expenses. When you do this, the inconvenience you suffer during the next month from having to save more than the normal amount will help to ensure that you do not repeat the mistake.

You should also be aware of things that make you spend a lot. If you have friends who come to take you clubbing every Friday night, and you always spend recklessly on drinks when you're out with them, you might want to avoid them. If you do go out, go with just a little cash and without your credit card. That way you can only order drinks for which you budgeted while you were still at home and sober.

Make your expectations realistic so you don't put too much pressure on yourself. Know that money stacking habits are a progressive activity that will need time to perfect. Do not get too frustrated with yourself when you don't meet your target. Just continue to try your best till you do meet it. Also make sure you're already comfortably meeting your last target, maybe two or three times consecutively, before setting a new one.

If you were making some progress but then got distracted and lost everything, you should start again at your beginnings. Start small and begin to build the habit and your savings again.

The Warren Buffet Example

When it comes to people who have used savings and investments to build wealth, no one compares to Warren Buffet. He is currently worth $73.3 billion, making him the fourth richest person in the world, with Bill Gates holding the top spot at $89 billion. When Warren Buffet was the second richest man in the world (sometime before 2010, when he was worth $31 billion, behind Bill Gates, who had $50 billion), he gave an hour-long interview on CNBC.

The highlight of the interview was when he told the story of how he bought his first share at the age of 11. He said that he regretted having bought the share too late; he should have bought it when he was 5. (He actually did buy six bottles of cola from his grandfather's grocery store when he was just six years old, reselling them for a 5% profit.)

The share he bought was from Cities Service, and it cost $38. He bought it for himself and his elder sister. After a short period of time, the share lost value and was worth only $27. However, he held onto it until it rose to $40, after which he sold it. This decision he also lived to regret, as the shares of Cities Service subsequently rose to $200. From this he learned to be patient with his investments.

He was able to save some money from delivering newspapers, which he used to buy a farm when he was just 14 years old. The share and the farm are example of investments he made even before he reached adulthood.

Despite being the second richest man in the world at the time of the interview, he was still living in a small 3-bedroom house he'd bought 50 years ago. He said that he had everything he needed inside the house. Even though the house didn't have a fence or a wall, he did not have security people around him. Neither did he have a driver; he drove himself anywhere he wanted to go to in his own car. Despite owning the largest private jet manufacturer in the world, he did not travel by private jet. He is therefore a great example of a modest personality.

He placed a priority on hiring the right person to manage each of the 63 businesses he owned. In line with this, he did not call them or meet with them regularly. He only wrote them a letter once a year. From this you can learn how important it is to employ the right people, for example if you are going to hire a stockbroker or financial advisor to manage your money. On the other hand, you should also only work in the right place, somewhere you are paid what you are worth to do what you are very good at doing.

Warren Buffet stated that his CEOs have only two rules. The first rule is that they should not lose any money belonging to shareholders in the business they manage. The second rule is that they should not forget the first rule. That shows a man of focus. You should also focus on your money stacking habits and make your first rule to save money, and your second rule not to forget the first rule.

He also stated in the interview that he goes home after work to watch television while eating popcorn instead of socializing. He did not have a computer or a mobile phone. This shows that he does not live beyond his income (or anywhere close to his income). He lives far below his income and avoids the temptation of living luxuriously by not mixing with people who would tempt him to spend more on luxurious things.

Here is some of Warren Buffet's other advice to young people on things that have helped him to achieve financial success:

- Stay away from debts and learn to develop yourself. This is in line with two of the habits discussed earlier relating to the disadvantages of being indebted and the advantages of investing in yourself.
- Man is not created by man, but money is created by man. This implies that to actually save or have money, you must consciously work towards it. It will be impossible to have money if you do not save money, no matter how much you earn.
- Live your life as simple as you are. This means that you should live a modest life, as explained above, and not try to live beyond your income or to create an impression by living a flashy lifestyle that you can't afford.

- Always do what you are happy about as opposed to doing what people say. When you try to follow or please people, you will be misled and you will lose money. You should learn to know what you want, what is best for you, and then do it. The reason a lot of people aren't successful is that they try to be like others. When they aren't able to be like those people, they get frustrated and they lose everything.
- Forget about brand names. Buy things you are comfortable with. When you buy things with famous names like Armani, Rolex and Samsung, you will be paying much more than the real value. You will be able to get cheaper alternatives of equal value. Go for the cheaper alternatives as long as they have everything that you need. Don't buy a phone worth $700 if all you're going to do with it is make calls and send text messages. A $20 phone can give you the same functionality and will probably have better battery life.
- It's wasteful to buy unnecessary things with your money. You should be more concerned about helping others in need. Warren Buffet wholeheartedly subscribes to the idea that philanthropy is a good money stacking habit. He is reported to have given over $30 billion to charity.
- Don't allow others to rule your life. When you give other people the power to rule your life, you will be wrongly advised and might be tricked into doing things that would be against your best

interests – and the money stacking habits you are trying to develop.

In another interview, Warren Buffet was asked if he was scared of higher interest rates or the war in Iraq. He said that at any given point in history, even in 1974, when stocks were very cheap, there were always a number of reasons why somebody could have decided not to invest in shares. He stated that nevertheless, the United States was doing well and that would be favorable for businesses. He went further to say that businesses in America have never really disappointed investors, but that investors have shot themselves in the foot any number of times. By this, he was probably referring to panic selling of shares during market downturns. Of course, the shares later rose to become profitable again.

Conclusion

It would be difficult to develop all of these money stacking habits overnight. First you should recognize which of them you already have and be sure that you are doing those properly. If there are some you are already working at, but have not perfected yet, start with those. Try to perfect them within a month or two. After that, you can start tackling the other habits you'd never tried to establish or weren't even aware of. For these habits, it's best to take them one after the other. If you try to rush all of them together, you might get overwhelmed and then just give up. List them in order of difficulty, start with the easiest ones, and add a more advanced one every month.

If you weren't practicing any of the habits before, you should have started developing all of them within two years. By the third year, you should have perfected them, and you will be surprised at how much you have saved already – and how much you will be saving on a yearly basis from now on.

You don't also have to start saving big the instant you begin. You will need to be strategic and start small. Attempting to start too big could destabilize and discourage you. If you optimum goal is to save 50% of your salary every month, but for now you're having to borrow money to tide you over until your next paycheck, your immediate goal should be ensuring that you start each month debt-free. Once you are able to achieve that in a month or two, then you can progress to saving 3 to

5% of your salary. Once that is achieved, you can, over the period of a year or two, approach your target of 50%.

For most people, though, the most they can comfortably save every month is between 25 and 30% of their income, which is still very decent. If you intend to save 30% of your income, you might want to budget 7% for emergencies, 10% for major expenses such as going on vacation, buying a car and building a house, and the remaining 13% for retirement savings. If you have any windfalls, you might want to put them toward major expenses so that you can become a homeowner more quickly.

www.ingramcontent.com/pod-product-compliance
Lightning Source LLC
Chambersburg PA
CBHW020454220526
45464CB00002B/984